Paincouragement

Paincouragement

Everything about life, inspiration,
and overcoming difficult times...
all in poetry

Amir Tavakkoli

Library of Congress Control Number:		2019920166
ISBN:	Hardcover	978-1-7960-7636-3
	Softcover	978-1-7960-7635-6
	eBook	978-1-7960-7634-9

To order additional copies of this book, contact:
Xlibris
1-888-795-4274
www.Xlibris.com
Orders@Xlibris.com
804580

TABLE OF CONTENTS

Introduction

Well, hello there. My name is Amir Tavakkoli and I am so glad you are reading my book. It is an honor and privilege that someone out there is reading my thoughts and words written on paper (or electronic device) and getting a glimpse into my life.

The purpose of this book, as the title suggests, is to discuss the typical things we deal in life, the difficulties of life, and to get the important life lessons out of them. To take the difficult times and turn them into something positive and use them as inspiration to improve and succeed in life. Most of them book is done in poetry format. Many personal experiences are included in it. Most of them have like a small paragraph or two, either at the beginning or at the end, which talk about the subject of the poem and the related life lesson to it.

Almost all the poems are general enough to where most of us can relate to them. The topics include, love and relationship (which is a big one), and relationships could be romantic, family, or even friends; it also includes things like the importance of compassion, keeping promises, mass shootings, even some politics, growing up in dysfunctional families, or with dysfunctional caretakers, drugs, and many other topics.

Let me tell you briefly about myself. I was born in Iran and came to the United States at age 13. It was hard in the beginning. Not knowing a word of English and being in a country where nobody can understand you, is not easy. On top of that, I came at a bad time. It was only a couple of months after the September 11 tragedy, and there were lots of unfair stereotype mistreatments towards people from the Middle East. I was called a terrorist, made fun of for not speaking English, picked on, lonely, and the list goes on and on. To make matters worse, my family life was also challenging. All the suffering turned me into someone I did not know existed in me, not in a good way. I turned to gang life, hung out with the wrong crowd, involved in daily physical fights, alcohol, drugs, etc. But all those experiences made me who I am today.

Thank God, my family and friends, and of course myself, I was able to turn my life around and get back on track. I finished law school and became a pretty successful lawyer. On the path of getting there, I had to overcome many more obstacles, a big one going through the difficulties of getting my United States citizenship (which I finally received), for something idiotic and minor I did when I was 18 years old. More details on that will hopefully be shared in a follow up book in the future. But had I known the things I know now (the stuff I preach in my book), then I probably would not have gone through such difficult times in the past. But like I mentioned, those experiences turned me into the person I am today, and they were the inspiration I needed to write this book.

If I can just inspire one person out there, to give a glimpse of hope, then my goal is accomplished. I want to thank all my family and friends, even those who are no longer a part of my life, my mentors, teachers, and everyone who cross my path in life, for making this book happen. I hope you enjoy!

"The Moment I Saw"

Topic: Love.

Ok, so the first poem is just purely about love. The feeling you get when you meet someone and something in your gut tells you this person can be the one. We get so excited and even without saying anything, people around us can tell something is different. Suddenly the world becomes a different place and you don't really know how you feel or how to express your feelings. This poem will be followed up with another one that is connected to it, so please keep close attention to some of the lyrics which will be restated in the follow up poem. Here is to hoping you find that person and stay with them forever.

A selfless smile
Full of purity, full of love!
Gentle soul & heart of gold
And eyes shining like the stars
Darker than the moonless night
Brighter than the radiant sun!
An innocent look, soft touch
In a life and body divine!

But recent stories of so many battles
And so many tides

The highs and the falls
Were hidden in your beautiful smile!
It's what drew me
To reach out, discover you,
To feel it all, to know it all
As my spirit stood tall!

To you, I was an unknown entity
Still unsure of who I was, who I am
Pondering the level of trust
You should give another man!
With so much to do lately
So much on your mind
Could it lead to, another disappointment or frown?
As you wondered, the level of trust
To give an unknown man!

Yet something inside, deep down
Gave you a sense of relief!
Satisfaction and joy, freed
Pound for pound, forever bound!
Mesmerizing, the sunrays shining
In all your cells, in every tingling drop
Dancing in the rain, in the autumn fall!
With fragrance of roses
All over your spirits, feelings
Going wild, surprised, also alarmed!

Maybe a crazy love story
That you've wanted for so long
A true love that you dreamed of
Since you were the adorable little child
Has finally come around
Like a lost friend, finally found!
--

Lost in the present
Imagination of the future
Gratitude for every moment, every chance

Every possibility, you passed in the past!
Intense sensation of pride, feeling proud!

Keep in mind, I got your back
In every step, every mishap, every delight
Walking along
On this journey we call life!
Uncovering what it's all about
The fascinating path!
Never to make you feel alone
Never looking back!

I may have been an unknown entity,
An unknown man
But from the moment I saw
Those dark beautiful eyes
Your breathtaking laugh, grounded smile
I knew you could be the one,
I can give love and support, unconditionally
Until the end of days
Until your heart desires
With a smile, hand by hand, side by side
Through every rise, every fall!

———wwwoooeroereoowww———

"Never, ever, ever, make you feel the same"

Topic: Acceptance, apology, and improvement in love.

The importance of apology! This one connects to the previous poem "The moment I saw".

You Promise to do something, but you fail. It's important to keep in mind that while you must own up to your mistake, apologize about it, and to do anything you can to <u>not</u> make same mistake; it is just as important to not beat yourself up about it too much. And the person that you are apologizing to should also generally be understanding and appreciate the fact that you are owning up to your mistake. Now, the level of trust may not be the same, but it's important to give people a chance to prove their improvements. Like stated, giving a chance doesn't necessarily mean having the same type of relationship. But when someone owns up to a mistake, apologizes and wants to fix the mistake, and you don't give that chance, there are a couple of issues that arise out of that. One, you would hurt the other person's self-esteem, because they may think "ok, I'll just keep doing the same, if this person I cared about so much for whom I apologized and owned to my mistake won't accept my apology, then what's the point to do the same for anyone else moving forward?"

Second, and more importantly, why it's important to accept an apology is because if you don't, you would hurt yourself as well. Forgiveness is always a beautiful thing because it shows your level of maturity when you aren't letting someone else's actions affect you and keep negative emotions inside you after they owned up to their mistake and apologized. So, communicate, let the person know how their words or actions affected your feelings.

Counting the days
I waited so impatiently and excitedly
For the time
To see your face
Lost in an unknown place, without a trace
Finally reached the destination,
Filled with grace,
From God
That life, the universe
Aligned the stars
For you and I, to meet
For me, to be your guest

That night, despite the fears
Despite the confusion and tears
The happiest man alive
I was
Completely amazed, and blown
Although, my actions and reactions
May not have shown
I must have more control

So, I must discuss
You see, my happiness, my joy inside
To be in your loving arms,
To be by your side
I might have disguised

For I was lost and mesmerized
As I warned, I may lose my legs and arms
When I see your beautiful eyes

Of all the things were said
I must admit the thing, that hurt the most
That had me lost,
Feeling like
The line, I crossed
Was my broken promise:

"To never make you feel alone"
You see, I made a choice, a pledge to be
A friend, a mate, support
"Until the end of days, until your heart desires"
"Hand by hand, side by side"
"Through every rise, and every fall"
Yet,
You felt alone
You felt, you had no one in this world
Missing your family in the cold

Although I tried, I failed
Tried to keep you warm and give support
To be, the one who made you whole
I failed
But we're only human

I hope, your heart and mind, align
To give it another try, another go
For I must show
That night, was a stepping stone
For me to learn, to earn
The right, to be by your side
And never, ever, ever, make you feel the same
Ashamed, I wait

—wooero叫eoom—

"Spiritual Prosperity"

Topic: Using struggle as inspiration to reach your full potential.

Sometimes in life, we go through certain things that take the soul out of us. At the time that we go through them, we may feel like nothing worse can be happening. The funny thing is most of the time, the severity of what we are dealing with, and how bad the situation seems, is not that bad; it's all in our heads.

The mind is an extremely powerful tool. We can choose to feel incredible in a difficult situation, filled with gratitude, at the same time we can take the most amazing experiences and times in our life, take them for granted, and not show any appreciation. The choice is ours and in our own heads. Everything passes, life goes on. So, sit back, relax, and enjoy the ride.

Summers come and go
Destiny, what I live for
With all my heart and soul
Faithful, that this life of mine
Is controlled by a higher power, more divine

I've had my moments, ups and downs
The journey, full of happiness, full of frowns, and downs!
I looked at the sky
Prayed, my chest pounding, heart going wild!

At the time, I was scared, petrified
Sunk in a valley of death
Darkness surrounded
With no way to climb

I searched, walked, ran, even dug
Under the torching sun
Sweating, hopeless, couldn't find a way
Getting back what was mine

Lord, would you help me?
I exclaimed with my last breath
Collapsed! felt a rapid force
Dashing though this body of mine

Suddenly changed,
My thoughts, my passion, vision
The force, helped me rise, helped me shine
Once again, I was alive

"Son, you've been wrong all along
Get up & visualize, the glory, the path
The valley? Not where you belong
You gotta help yourself
Before it's said and done
Nobody will help you
Not a man, not a dime.
Contagious jealousy, evil thoughts
All they want, is your shrine."

As the voice vanished
My eyes opened wide
No more sorrow, no pain
And the scars gone
A clear mind, wisdom, faith
Will take me far!

Back to the top, where I belong
The valley, was imaginary
All in disguise

"Never let sorrow or pain bring you down. Use it as power and motivation to get you where you belong, to shine, in *Spiritual Prosperity!*"

"Promises"

Topic: The effects of broken promises on our loved ones.

Ok, so this next poem is about keeping our promises. Sometimes, we may promise something in the moment to just get us what we are wanting or asking for, and we fail to consider the effects that it could have on the other person that we are making the promise to.

Many of us don't even understand or honor what a promise is and how strong of a commitment it is or should be. In my opinion, we should always, always think about the possible effects and pain that breaking a promise could cause to the other person, or in legal terms, the effects it could have on the "promisee", before making a promise. Almost one hundred percent of the time, the benefit of getting what you want at the moment by making a false promise and then breaking it is not worth the pain, confusion, and anger caused not only to the other person, but also to the relationship as a whole. With that said, I dedicate this to my family and friends for any promises I have made to them that I failed to keep. I love you.

———∿∾⟨∾⟩∿⟨∾⟩∾∿———

Promises I made
In moments of pain
To get you to stay
Were far from fair

Like a flower in the fall
Your pedals one by one
Fell to the ground and died
With every promise, unkept

Slowly they went, kissing the dirt
With prayers as they sank, prayers all around
Prayers afloat
Prayers as they burned

I could feel your sorrow
I could feel the hurt
I could feel your torpor
I could see you burnt

But never in a thousand years
I could imagine you dead
Never in a blue moon
I imagined life, without you
Feeling ashamed

Breaking point, was its turning point
Heartless and self-aware
What the flower needed
To protect its life
Protect its root

Hope remained, life inside
Roots in the ground
Until once again, spring comes

As the last pedal detached
I finally understand
My broken promises
Took the aroma, softness, in the dirt
As I took another chance

I reached my hands
As far as I could
Attempted to make a stance
To keep the promises, I had

To return the beauty where it belonged
A broken heart, took me by surprise
Took my breath away, shocked
The flower had already, relapsed

Spring will come, one more time
New pedals, will return
The roots are still alive

So relentlessly I work
With promises rejuvenated
Rest assured, dedicated I will be
With all my heart, my soul, and life
To the resurrection of your pedals
So that once again, you will come

Happy, bright, full of love
Seeing I kept my promises
For once
While you were gone!

You have always been there for me no matter what. Even when
I allowed your pedals to fall; when I didn't protect you; when I
didn't give you kindness; when I forgot about you, or failed to
give you water so that your bright colors and amazing fragrance
can shine all the time, your roots always remained strong. And
protected me at all times."

Forever grateful to you! I love you!

"They struggled, they conquered"

Topic: Civil rights heroes and continuing their legacy.

This next poem is about civil rights; about those people who sacrificed everything so that everyone else can enjoy a better life. Sometimes we forget about these people and how much easier they made life for the rest of us. May their souls rest in peace. And thank you for everything you did for us.

As I was walking in the middle of the night
I couldn't help but to think about the people who have fought
Fought the great war for civil rights;
Lost many battles
But did not lose the war

Oh, how brave were these young men and women?
Sitting in front of a bus
Rosa Parks sure knew how to fuss.
Martin Luther King was not afraid of jail
As he knew about Mahatma Ghandi
Who did not fail
Malcom X, Harriet Tubman, Booker Washington

And so many other greats have come and gone
But their legacies are still with us
As I am walking through the dawn

I must not forget Abraham Lincoln
For without him
I would be sitting in the south sinkin

Oh I have been walking for a long time
But thinking about these angels
Has me feeling fine.
That there are people in the world who truly care
People who would refuse to eat
So that you and I can share

Share the breath of life
The breath of freedom
If you do not know about these angels
You must see them.
Just take a look around, they're everywhere
I can feel their presence
Even in my prayers

As the sun approaches the sky
I wonder if some-day
I will be able to fly
I wonder if some day
I will be able to say:
    "I continued your legacy, now it's another angel's turn."

I am getting the hang of the shadows
Feeling almost prepared
I can proudly say:
They struggled, they conquered

"Mass shootings"

Topic: The importance of constantly remembering and working on resolving the issue of mass shootings.

What can I say? Mass shootings. My fingers get weak when I try to write or type about mass shootings, so I'll just let you read the poem.

A cold and rainy night
Blankets covering their fictitious arms
And a false sense of being in power
A false sense of doing what's right
Has 'em all hyped up
For only a few days of media, stirring the pot

They pray as they prepare
For a bloody and heartless day
Filled with blood and hurt
Confusion, calling it bravery and a just fight
Feeling completely motivated, but lost

Lost in a world so incompassionate
Shooting holes in bodies, with an unthinkable rate

Complete lack of affection to prevent
Families torn apart, and dreams burnt

No sense of love, minds filled with commotion
They move in pointless direction
Connection, to God, or belief in a higher power,
To which they have no affiliation

Dressed in dark gear, in fooling ways
The doors kicked open with grueling fears
Loudly and clear, here comes the hate
The lack of understanding, they never gained when raised
And lived in a state of mental sickness, unchanged
Brainwashed to the point of being dead

As they scramble scared
The shocked civilian lives,
Are running down the stairs
Looking for a place, to run away and hide
Their fear and tears

Political views suddenly disappeared and drained
As the heartbeats race
In a scene filled with shattered dreams
Causing forever lasting nightmares

Post chaos and all the mess
For only a few days,
Suddenly we care
For only a few days
We discuss change, and who's to blame

And then,
So easily and carefree
We forget and continue to be
Self-centered, unchanged
Forgetting the lives taken heartlessly, burned in a blaze

The hearts that were meant to be
That were meant to see
So much more,
Blind-sided they will always be!

"Where were you?"

Topic: Children living and raised in dysfunctional families.

This next poem is about issues caused to children who are born and raised in dysfunctional families. Dysfunctional as it relates to families is a term I learned from this book I have been reading about how to grow emotionally and mentally.

I pray for a day that all parents or caretakers gain more knowledge about how to raise children, and how mental and emotional well-being are far superior in the level of importance as compared to physical well-being. Unfortunately, most parents and caretakers believe if they provide food and a roof for their children, they are doing a good job; a completely ignorant and inaccurate belief in my opinion.

———————————

For every nasty smell of a cigarette
For every unkept promise
Every night spent without your presence
Every game played without your help

For every night sitting by the sidewalk impatiently waiting
Every school performance only imagining you cheering

Every situation I needed fatherly healing
Every broken wall, every leak in the ceiling

Every blue rainy night
For every time I had to see you behind bars
Every tear dropped down your face, you called pink eyes
Every holiday without you by my side
And every wish to have your hands in mine

Every fight, I didn't want
And every time I was confused
And needed to know what was right
Every missed flight
And every broken heart
I needed your advice

For all the pain, the confusion, and all the shame
For the lack of being properly trained
A tear dropped down my face
And raced,
Down a river,
Creating a hopeless imaginary ocean

I wish you were there
To at least help me swim
While I cried for help
As I drowned in sorrow and hate:

The hate for every family dinner and birthday cakes
For every performance I was late
Waiting on you, begging the Lord for a break
So that just for one night
As a family, we can celebrate

The hate for every child spoiled by their dad
Causing me countless fights, sometimes I wish I never had
The hate for a father and son ice cream date
God knows I wanted it so bad

Dad, I may never let you see
What you caused this person to be
During so many years you were too gone and carefree
While I struggled to find who I was, to find me

But I must free, my thoughts
You see,
The pen and paper is all I got
To help me survive,
To release the tension and provide
A coping mechanism, a ride
For all fatherless children around the world
To hop on,
Know they're not alone
And maybe make them feel a little bit alive

Who else is gonna listen and not
Be judgmental and careless,
And let us not rot?
Who will be the shoulders to cry on,
When neither your mom or dad would sacrifice

As a spectator, you could have been the one
To help that playful, smart, kind child
Actually be a child!
But no matter where I looked,
I gained and found everything,
Yet you, I couldn't find

I forgive you dad, I forgive myself
For every night you weren't there,
And I blamed myself
I forgive you because you didn't know better
But I must release, all the tension and disbelief
To be a batter man, for my own son, at ease

You're here now
Forget the past

Let's start over and blast
The music of life, and dance!

━━━ww~o~Q~o~Q~o~Q~o~ww━━━

This is dedicated for all the children out there not having a present father (or mother), and wondering "why"? For all the children crying to God why they cannot have a normal and loving family. For all the children blaming themselves for their parents' immaturity and lack of family unity. I want to put this out there in the universe for you, even though you may not read it until later in your life, so you know that you're not alone; that you're not the blame. You see, you're just a little child. You were not brought in this world on your own decision. It was your parents who made the decision to bring you in this world. So why should you be the one responsible to learn it on your own? You're not.

And parents, remember these words: they're only a child. You cannot expect them to learn things on their own; stop punishing them, blaming them, or even doing everything for them, but guide them instead. Show them the ways for learning their emotional and mental maturity, but don't travel the road for them. Even though I understand sometimes separation is the only solution, remember that your child is 50% of your own reflection. So next time you badmouth your child's father or mother in the presence of your child, the wounds and the pain caused, is really damage caused to yourself. Remember that while the former spouse you so much hate, may not be your lover or anymore your mate, that person is still the father or mother of your own child, so you must be at your best.

"Sisterly love"

Topic: The love shared between siblings.

Siblings; how amazing are they? When I was a child growing up, my main wish was to always have a brother or sister. God later blessed me with a half-sister and a half-brother when I was older. But to have a brother or sister growing up with you is a blessing that we should always cherish. Here is to that life-long best friend we call sibling.

———⚬⚬⚬⚬⚬⚬⚬⚬———

She came in my life
Gave me wings
Filled my heart with laughter
Helped me sing

To dance in the rain
What she gave to me
Seeing her beautiful eyes
It's how she sang to me
Oh, she sang to me.

I couldn't believe it
What a feeling
Soulmates from the start
Even when apart.

Designed for love and healing
A blessing received
Got me on my knees, got me kneeling
Her love, oh so appealing.

Gentle as they come
Her soul, so divine
Pure, full of love
Always by my side, never gone
Delicate and calm
Swimming like a swan.

Sometimes I wonder
Could I live one moment
Without her?
As I've been so drawn
To this beautiful white swan.

"Lost in your tenacious world"

Topic: Toxic relationships.

Ok, so this one has mixed feelings for me. Toxic relationships are bittersweet. They are sweet because you have someone who is by your side. And even though the relationship may be toxic, we still feel some appreciation because we think "well, at least there's someone there who puts up with everything next to me." While that may be a good feeling, we must determine whether the good feeling is worth the effects of the toxicity and fighting of the relationship. It is an extremely hard decision to make. We often fail to even be able to make that determination or decision because we get so attached and used to the other person being around. Detachment should be practiced daily. This is a concept I must practice more myself as I often find myself getting attached, whether it's to a family member, friend, partner.

Attachment issues are often caused by some childhood experience. Usually it is caused by not having a stable family, absent parents, or parents who were not able to provide mental and physical support for children. Physical support includes the need for affectionate touching. Too much of it is a problem just as much as not enough of it is a problem. Parents who do not know their boundaries when it comes to providing the need for physical affection to their children, often find themselves behind bars for inappropriate sexual contact with their children; in some extreme cases there are parents who marry and have a child with their own child, sickening it is. These children end up either being so vulnerable that they either do not know how to stop someone from touching them and think that it is okay for anyone to take advantage of their bodies, because it "feels good", or they end up being so scared of everyone that even when they find a partner who truly loves them, they are afraid and paranoid to have any sexual or physical contact, even if it's an innocent hand holding.

On the other hand, there are parents who do not provide any physical affection to their children at all. All children need to be given physical affection. The human body produces chemicals by physical touch that make us feel safe and loved. When children do not get any appropriate physical touch and affection, they often grow up being needy for physical touch and end up getting it any way they can, without respecting their own or the other person's boundaries.

Mental support basically boils down to finding a balance between guiding your kids to do the right things, without involvement of inappropriate punishment, versus giving them too much freedom. Inappropriate levels of punishment can destroy a child's self-esteem in the long run and either turn them into either bullies, or weak to the point of not being able to stand up for themselves.

Okay I am getting off topic here, back to the poem, toxic relationships, I hope you enjoy it.

I wanted to be a good man
But you were almost undeserving.
Wanted to be loving and tender, to be stable
But you were traversing
In all directions
Countless reactions and imitations
Attempting to satisfy your tenacious sensations

I was lost in a world so cruel
In your tendencies to limit my salvation

25

Worn-out and almost robotic
I became lost without notice
And you allowed it, without much of a fight,
Almost without hesitation!

For so long, I took everything I could
Let pride and self-esteem take beatings so shrewd
So your desires and needs, could
Lead the show, unaffected, unshook!
Selfless and unaware, like a beast acting lewd
I became the masterpiece of your unforgiving selfish world!
Hopeless, and rendered weak in destitute.

For so long, I let you be my world
Took all the pain, the blame, the shame, the tame
So you could feel the fame, the gain, and refrain
From all the things, that cause tension and hurt
It got me burned
Next to me, in an unstoppable fire
You were also, burnt!

Don't get me wrong, I was partially to blame
Supposedly, it was all my fault
And probably, admittedly, I was mainly to blame
But sacrifice and compromise, things we couldn't apprehend

I pray the Lord, for nothing but success
For you and I, to be blessed
In a world full of accomplishments and praise
What's left,
And learn from our mistakes

I've had enough of all the weight, placed
On these lowered and fallen shoulders
That once again are whole, are raised
Time to cherish the rest!
And cherish what we witnessed

―∿∾⟳⟲∿―

"Space in a relationship"

Topic: The importance and positive outlook on giving space in a relationship.

"I need some space".

How many of you have heard that before? I can tell you personally I have, and it is not fun. Our first reaction is always to freak out. Thus, what we do is we act out of emotion immediately and really don't think things through. Then after we have said all the stupid things we could say, and the relationship has either been extremely damaged or ended, we come to our senses afterwards. We then have so much work to do to make up what has been damaged, if it's even possible to repair it anymore. But regardless, we can always take something positive out of seeking space in a relationship. There are plenty of YouTube videos and information out there about it on the internet, but I've never really seen in explained in poetry, so here it comes.

Patience, a virtue I've lacked
Going crazy and insane
Every time I had the chance
To use the tools, given and enhance
My life, growth, suppose, it's just a class

Consider it opportunity,
A time to blast
Exceed in life, succeed, proceed, advance
Without a doubt, at last I'll dance
Without a doubt, this time I'll pass

Seeking space, what you asked
Promise, that this will only last
A time brief, to use for grief
To remove confusion, stress release

But also,

A time to be, confused and feel
My loss, my heart, my words, you miss
In every key you hit
In every tone, and sound you create
On the keyboard you play
In every thought, you're bound to relate
To me
you see, it's not me you played
It's us, for which you cared

So you could:

Use the space to find, your only self
In a time, where life cannot be traced
Trying to find your ways,
In this new place you're faced!
So use the time, you know who you are
The one who provides, compassion and grace

And while, at the time you asked, I was confused and hurt
I was blind, couldn't find, the points relayed
In a state of sadness, I was raged

Or maybe, what you will see
Is this wasn't meant to be

Not what I wish for
But God's plan,
I won't question or tease
As in the end, we will both have peace

For now, I know
I must grow
I must be the man you want and know,
The man I know
And let it show
Not the one who would refuse
To show respect and blows his fuse
For a simple request, it's just different views
In the end, both of us better and ready
To give and take, but this space
It's pleasantly shitty
But a reminder to be friendly and steady

"Don't take the doll"

Topic: Damaged woman who no longer believes.

Not to be sexist here, this also applies to men. I used "damaged woman" in the topic because when I wrote the poem, it was a woman I was thinking of.

Sometimes we go through experiences in life that make us lose faith. We believe, but bad experiences keep happening and we end up quitting and lose faith in humanity and love. Remember what we experience and how we look at it is all in our minds. As I stated in the poem, *Spiritual prosperity*, "we can choose to feel incredible, and filled with gratitude, in a difficult situation, or we can take the most amazing experiences and times in our life, take them for granted, and not show any appreciation; the choice is ours and in our own minds. Everything passes, life goes on." I hope all of us remain positive, believe, and keep faith. It may feel like you can never catch a break, but that's the beauty of life.

———∽∽∾⊙⟋⊙∿∿———

Playing on a small playground
She was laughing and smiling, like a doll!
I've heard it all before
I've seen it all before
Of a life changed,

In a few moments, caught off guard
Insulting the matter of time!

Suddenly a storm,
Came rushing down
Took her by surprise
Destroyed the playground
Of the little child!
Her smile, long gone
Nowhere to be found!

"NO! NO! NO! Leave her alone"
I shouted at the storm, shouted at the gods!
"Let the child play, enjoy the breeze
she's just a sinless little doll!"
"Don't take her away,
Don't turn another soul,
Cold, from all the pain!
For she brings joy,
She brings light,
To this world of ours, to broken hearts!"

This can't be real,
This can't be the end
It's not what she wants
She's just a child!
With so much life ahead
So much life to live
So much to find!

Reminiscing the old days,
Bright colors, chalked on the ground
With only tears in her eyes
She remembered the storm
The merciless roaring sound
Destroying her every belief
Her imaginations, her sense of being alive!
Losing her faith in love!

"You're the only one
That can bring out the sun!
You're the only one who knows
How to take the storm and turn it into a jewel!
For her, to once again be
That cute little child
That cute little doll!
To once again see,
The beauty in the sky
The beauty of love!"

Little girl, don't let a split second go by
Cruise though it all
The shortcomings and the falls!
The storm can't take you down
Or shatter your dreams, imaginations, feelings
For we all have a beautiful soul
In the heavens above
To be our guiding hands!

"For Once in Our Lives"

Topic: Compassion.

Compassion is a forgotten human value. Often, we see people struggle and we simply look away and ignore it. We think "oh, just like I had to work hard to get to where I am, so can they." Or we see people who are sick, have cancer, or struggling with mental issues, and we simply don't care. We fail to consider other people and the struggles they are dealing with, because we are dealing with our own. We fail to have understanding that it may not be poor work habits, it may be severe mental issues that prevents them from keeping, or even getting a job. Some people just haven't learned how to communicate, how to fill out an application, or to even ask for a job. Society has extremely limited resources for these individuals, contrary to popular belief. We fail to realize it isn't drugs that is destroying people, it's the underlying issues that turned those people to drugs that are the real issue.

Please have compassion, give a smile, help someone you can. What you give to the world, it gives back to you. The more you give, the more you receive' I strongly believe that.

———❦———

Passing by, watching the homeless man beg
Passing by, watching the little child cry

Watching the mother selling roses
Begging for a dollar, just to get by
Passing the children with cancer, stuck in despair
Not throwing a smile
Throwing thorns and stones, as they slowly die

What have we become? Tell me why
For once in our lives
We can't be children of God
That man with no legs
Believed, when he put his life on the line
Believed in you and I

The woman whose face was splashed
Had dreams of becoming a star
But the acid, it only left scars
Scars?
How about her whole face, gone!

For once in our lives,
Let's be selfless, let's not simply pass by!
Give the homeless man hope, just a notch
Give him your soul, your touch!
Seeing the boy cry? Sit by his side
Let the tears dry

Children with cancer, stuck in despair?
Give them kindness, with a smile
A reason for their wounds to repair!
The thorns and stones? Keep em
Throw them far away
A place, no one can reach em

For once in our lives, let's be thankful
For the legs we spare
Be thankful, for your beautiful face
Black, white, brown
Regardless of race

The acid? Left everlasting results
Color we worry about? What a disgrace

Wake up! Smell the roses
Breathe the air, we enjoy in limitless doses
For once in our lives,
Let's make the world better
Let's make it a better place
Loaded with devotion!

"Mothers are like trees"

Topic: The loving and giving nature of mothers.

Mothers, just wow. I have not been blessed to have a child yet. But I am sure that once God willing I do, I will be much more appreciative of what it is like to be a parent. My mother has had a tough life trying to raise me. She has dealt with two difficult marriages. She often worked three jobs at the same time just so she can keep a roof on my head. I didn't appreciate it at the time as much as I should have and failed to realize how difficult it is for her to have done that. I was in a really difficult time of my life between the ages of 16-18 years old. While thanks to her and her full commitment and support at all times, I was able to get my life back together, I had to deal with other personal issues between the ages of 24 and 30 years old. My mother never left my side and always supported me. I don't always agree with her style of parenting or communication, but I know she has a pure heart and 100% committed to see my happiness and success.

Here is to all the mothers out there, who I compare to trees for their unconditional love and support; they are truly "majestic."

Drops of rain
Memories Slain
Pictures of love and gain
Dancing aflame
In mesmerizing ways!

Call it revelation, call it ablaze
Scorching the earth
Unaltered, unphased!
Innocent and true
In what they believe
Strong and patient
It's what they've been trained!

Magnificent lives
Protecting our days
Standing high,
Full of power
Full of grace
Full of strength!
Leaving no-one behind
Selfless and unpraised!

Like mothers as they raise
Their lovely children
Selfless and unpraised!
Strong as they go
Majestic and kind
Just like the trees
They give life away
Yet content and unphased!

"Another broken heart"

Topic: Broken hearts.

Broken hearts are not fun to deal with. We feel physical pain in the body when we deal with a broken heart. It literally feels broken, and what makes it so difficult to deal with is that nothing other than "time" fixes it. At the time we deal with a broken hear, we fail to recognize and understand the magic word, time, that time will heal everything.

The good news is that as painful as a broken heart may feel, it isn't like any other sickness for which we don't know what the end-result will be, whether we will be healed or not. Time always heals a broken heart, as long as we remember that, and live life and take it one day at a time. During the difficult time of suffering a broken heart, we must focus on ourselves, expand our horizon, stay busy, pick up something new, turn to art, etc.

The bad news is that a broken heart not only affects us physically with the induced pain, it also drains us emotionally. Something like a broken leg (which I have happened to experience, a severe broken femur), typically only has physical pain, but usually no emotional damage. But a broken heart also severely damages us emotionally. Some people get extremely depressed, lose faith, and are never the same person as they once were.

Stay positive, remember time ALWAYS heals a broken heart; and you WILL be whole again. You will find your true love, either the same person, who with time will be a more complete and better version of themselves when they come back or someone new who is better. Keep faith, stay strong, and live life while enjoying the ups and downs. In the end, it is not in reaching the destination that we get joy out of life, but in the events that happen on the path of getting there.

———∿∽⊙⌒⊙⌒⊙∽∿———

As I sit here in this lonely shattered world
I take a look around and remember the good old days
The days of laughter and joy
The butterflies flying majestically in our small
But complicated worlds
The nervousness of the first time we talked
And all the minutes and seconds
I waited by the phone to see your call
Every moment, every minute, was worthwhile
To get only a chance
Another hello,
Even if the end was a goodbye

Now I'm sitting here
With another broken heart
Not thinking "what if" or what I did wrong
What we did wrong
But thankful that we tried

In a time where love is lost
Days in which
People no longer believe, don't give a fuck
Two beautiful people in the world
You and I
Gave love a chance,
And can happily say we tried

Maybe it's just me seeing the good in you
Or seeing the good in us
But I'll live with that
No matter how many times
I try and take a loss
No matter how many broken hearts

Because once again I will love
I will give it another try
Time after time
Fall flat on my face, and again I will rise

To show the world
Not all hope is lost
That what you seek, you shall find
I believe
Even in the moments I cry
Even when at the lowest point of them all

"Different than the rest"

Topic: Trust your instinct of love.

Instinct! A lost human feeling that God has provided since the day we are born, and it remain within us until we die. The issue is that the longer we live and the older we get, the more we forget and disregard our instincts. Society has set so many rules and expectations about what is right and what is wrong, what we should do and shouldn't do, who we should pursue and shouldn't pursue, what we can achieve and can't achieve, etc, that the more we live and learn, the more we develop, the more we fail to trust our instinct.

What society fails to realize, what our friends and family fail to realize, is that every situation is different, every person is different, every outcome is different. This is what makes us individually beautiful and incredible. This is the reason God created us all differently, with different looks, different feelings, different emotions, different set of strengths and weaknesses, different experiences, different lives; even twins are never the exact same individual. If everything was already pre-determined as society portrays it to be, then what would be the meaning of life? What would be the meaning of trying? What would be the meaning of having goals and dreams and pursuing them?

Trust your instinct! Go with what your heart tells you, not what family, friends, mentors, famous people, or anyone else tells you. Just make sure you don't pursue what your instinct tells you in an illegal way.

You never know what someone is going through, you never know what is happening in the universe, you never know why something is happening the way it is. Don't let society or other people dictate what you do and what your God given instincts tell you. Be yourself, trust yourself, and have faith.

Thinking I'm just another mistake
You smile beautifully and walk away
Leaving this heart behind
Letting our love slide
"Trust me you say"
I hope you're right

Feelings of regret
Fill your mind with so many thoughts
Causing a headache
You can't get rid of
As if you're left behind bars

Caged up and lonely
Both of us in confusion now
Come back to me slowly
You ask how or why?
Because,

I'm not used to having my heart left broken
Or feeling all shaken
Up, didn't wanna see myself woken
From the amazing dream you instigated!
Forsaken, from
Leaving all these emotions and feelings
Unattended
And so many words you've left unspoken

Every part of me
Is holding on

To every part of you
Every joy in me
Is holding on to
Waiting to see
Every lovely smile of you

I pray love finds a way
To find in us
A place to stay awhile
Hoping forever
Feeling like a lost child
Can't stop thinking
Continuously chasing
What I found in you

Now I debate if I'm left with every photo of you
Every thought of you
Feeling you in my soul, maybe I was wrong
Hearing you in every song

Like a broken record
Roaming around in circles
Until my last breath
Until I shatter every record

It was only just a breath away
Only another soft touch away
So don't let go of the grace
We've been given, and embrace
Rather than
Thinking of me as another mistake

We're only getting older
Rest your head on my shoulder
Make the waiting time pass by quicker
Help my heart no longer be a quitter

Let me show you why you thought I am different than the rest
For you only deserve the best
And while I may be far from it,
I'm certainly different than the rest
For you I'll win every race
Or collapse with my last breath!

"How many times?"

Topic: Stopping war worldwide.

This is one of those heartbreaking topics that I get teary eyed writing about. Since I was a child, I remember I would always wonder why there were innocent kids dying in war. I would question God and why God was allowing for it to happen. I always believed in God since I remember, but seeing children die in the middle of a war always gave me doubts and raised questions like "what kind of God would allow for this happen?" While I still have not found the answer to that question, my belief and love for God has not changed, I believe in God even more and my belief and faith is stronger than before. I do have the added advantage and belief now that "everything happens for a reason!". While I cannot think of a good reason why children should die in war, I no longer seek the answer from God. I know now there are many things in life we don't understand, but there is a purpose behind everything.

I pray for the day that war no longer exists. I pray for a day that innocent lives are no longer lost for power, for political reasons, or for disagreements between people and countries. That day, that day my friend will be the day we all witness heaven on earth.

How many times until the rain stops?
Until the soldiers sojourn, taste the buds?
Without a worry on their minds
They count the stars!
Daylight seems so far away
And hope is only a minute too far

Yes, we have come along
We have passed the shining walls, the fails and the falls
They believe we can rise...

The beating shoes inside a tint
And the mother worried about the rent
The child shivering in the snow,
Wondering when daddy will be home
Only a few minutes too long

How many times will blood clot?
The red, covering their boots
The guns, tanks, children, dead
It's only a matter of time
Tell me, how many times?

How many times will I drop a tear?
River, sea, ocean
Do you now realize that the gun is real?
Cannot fathom, this is happening
I wake up and my dreams are catching up
A wet towel over the face, raiser, mirror
The blood runs down my face
And I realize, it has all been real

How many times until I get you to stop?
To understand, learn, grow
That this is all real?
To cherish the plates, bread, sun
This is all temporary
Power has only begun

But will it end?
How many times until we clinch that it will end?
None!
The end is not near

"*Dear anonymous*"

Topic: Growing up with dysfunctional caretakers.

I have written previously on this issue. The explanation and life lessons and concepts behind it are almost identical to what I wrote in the poem "Where were you?" Please refer that that poem. We can also apply the following excerpt from the poem "Lost in your tenacious world":

"Attachment issues are often caused by some childhood experience. Usually it is caused by not having a stable family, absent parents, or parents who were not able to provide mental and physical support for children. Physical support includes the need for affectionate touching. Too much of it is a problem just as much as not enough of it is a problem. Parents who do not know their boundaries when it comes to providing the need for physical affection to their children, often find themselves behind bars for inappropriate sexual contact with their children; in some extreme cases there are parents who marry and have a child with their own child, sickening it is. These children end up either being so vulnerable that they either do not know how to stop someone from touching them and think that it is okay for anyone to take advantage of their bodies, because it "feels good", or they end up being so scared of everyone that even when they find a partner who truly loves them, they are afraid and paranoid to have any sexual or physical contact, even if it's an innocent hand holding.

On the other hand, there are parents who do not provide any physical affection to their children at all. All children need to be given physical affection. The human body produces chemicals by physical touch that make us feel safe and loved. When children do not get any appropriate physical touch and affection, they often grow up being needy for physical touch and end up getting it any way they can, without respecting their own or the other person's boundaries.

Mental support basically boils down to finding a balance between guiding your kids to do the right things, without involvement of inappropriate punishment, versus giving them too much freedom. Inappropriate levels of punishment can destroy a child's self-esteem in the long run and either turn them into either bullies, or weak to the point of not being able to stand up for themselves."

You must look at me now
With everything I got
And think you're proud
Of the man I've become

For bank accounts and fancy lawn
The rise
From being the little boy who lived with no roof
From going block to block
And fight to fight to pay dues
To a young man, whose only plan
Ever was to run loose

Now take another look
Are you really proud?
As you scream aloud

From all the pain, the rain, the gain, the bane, you called tools
To all the blame, the shame, the game, the claim remained the
same:
To keep me sane

Of all the cars, the bars, the rise, flaws remained
Because my feelings,
Were never trained

The beating and bleeding and yelling and blaming
Caused harm preventing me to reach my ceiling
To be who I wanna be
As a human being

Don't get me wrong,
I'm not blaming you
You didn't know better
As I wrote in the unsent letters

But I hold you accountable
This was preventable
Now we've reached the inevitable
The deep scars inside
Would only take awhile
To try
And run, to die, as all they've known
As all they've done
Was cry inside, and hide
The tears, and fly afar
But it was only a matter of time

To reach, the destiny I face
The place, I call
The final show
The last stage

But no, it's time to grow, to flow
These feelings can't stay

Allow the rain, to wash it all away
To learn and claim
My only life, can only be brave, and never cave
To free the slave, I hide
Embrace the life, I got
And never make the same mistakes!

"Dear life"

Topic: Getting a second chance; personal auto accident experience.

This is about a personal auto accident experience I had in which I flipped my car while falling behind the wheel driving at 3 o'clock in the morning. But applied more broadly, it is about having a second chance in life. I can tell you there have been at least a few incidents in life where I could have, should have, been wiped off this earth. But I was given another chance. At the time of this accident, I was seventeen years old, I was at a very dark place in my life.

We can always use our past experiences to appreciate life more. I never regret anything I did in the past, no matter how bad it was. If I could turn back time and start over, I would probably do many things differently, but I don't have any regrets. All my experiences, the good and the bad, all my flaws and strengths, make me the person I am today. And I am proud of who I am.

—————

Dear life, I love you, but I hated you
With bullets on the ground
No-one knows my struggles
As car flipped upside down

Now riding the greyhound

I was not alone at first
But my "friend"
He was resting in his place
Resting under the white sheets
Covering his sins

Dazed off, in an alternative world
Going all over
All over the globe
With alcohol and weed
My sensations were getting raised

But no more BAC, to keep me awake
The nasty stuff, was all I had left
As broke as I was
Unlike the other guys
In their fancy cars

Angry at the world
Daddies were what they got
Gave them everything
And all I ever wanted
Was just another night
With my daddy by my side
But fascinating dreams
Were all I ever got

As I fell asleep
In a gentle blink
My soul was taken out
My body was feeling weak
Spirit going wild

And suddenly I was
Trapped in a ditch
Deeper than my own height

Sadder than goodbye
Hitting rock bottom and feeling terrified
Like most my worthless life
Like after every crime

Eyes open wide
Yet, only in sight
Tears running down my face
Lord please help me survive

Disbelief in the scene
Shattered all my dreams
"How did I survive?"
I was thinking, as I walked it off
But still dead inside
Weeping nonstop
Until the pain felt numb

Begging to the Lord
With feelings of repent
But it was just another lie
To get to me to survive
With every tear dropped
Felt heavier than a rock
Hit the ground and killed
My imagination and dreams

Lord, just another chance
All I ever want

"Satanic Struggles"

Topic: Dealing with difficulties of the world.

We all have them, evil thoughts. This is about my evil thoughts. Don't let them take control because they can, easily, in a matter of moments. I know because they took control over me in the past. And they probably still do, but to a much lesser extent. I have learned to manage them better and not let them take me over. Don't let your evil thoughts take control. Don't speak while you are angry, don't make promises when you are happy, and don't judge while you are disappointed.

For all the speechless mountains
The chaotic rivers
The phony smiles
And the diverting goodbyes

For every handshake blown
Every thought unspoken
The magic tricks and all
They were all just ideas, grown

My life, hasn't been the painless glow
My life, hasn't been a fancy show
Snacking on the crumbles thrown

I've tasted the junk, felt torn and blown

My life, it's been a seductive show
Jumping through the wild woes
Hear my thoughts explode
With a wild prose, taking the role

From the gang life to fancy rows
Roofless homes to mansions
Junk yard cars to Gallardos and Benz
Maniacs posing as lovers exposed
Clothes not a poor child on earth could pose

But a fake smile always worn, as I rose
Deep inside, the struggle
A reality unfit for the world
Senseless temptations and unforgiving world

It's been a satanic compilation
Yet the march goes
Without hesitation
For the seductive scene
That a time or few, my eyes have seen.

"Wrong definition of strength"

Topic: When men cry. Also, the misdirected classification of honor based on the work you do.

Ok this poem gets very personal for me. But the topic is the unfair judgment and humiliation men get when they cry. Often when society sees a man crying, and unless it is for watching the movie "The Notebook", it isn't considered "romantic". It is considered a weakness. When a man cries, (not to be sexist but women specially tend to do this more than men) people consider that he isn't "man enough", that he can't have a family, or that he isn't strong enough. But have we ever considered that men and women are both human? That men have the same feelings as women? The same fears as women? The same insecurities as women? The same human emotions as women? The same questions as women?

Yes, we live in a world where men are expected to be emotionless, while women are expected to show too much emotion. We are all human.

This poem is about an incident that happened to me. It was after a separation, in which I couldn't help but cry. She is an amazing person and helped me get through so much in life for which I am forever thankful to her. At the time of the separation,

I showed the only reaction I had left for when all hope of keeping the relationship intact was gone. But I was accused of being weak for having cried, from different people. Although at the time I was such an emotional wreck that maybe I believed them, that maybe I was weak, deep down I knew I wasn't. My response was "if you consider my crying weak, because I so deeply don't want to end the relationship, and because I feel I have no control over it anymore, then consider me the weakest man in the world." To this day I still believe that. Crying shows you care; it shows you are committed; it shows you are hurt; it shows you are human. In fact, after I was able to get through the grieving process, I came to my senses and realized that the opposite is true. Take a moment to consider this:

> If you <u>don't cry</u> as a man (or a woman) when you are extremely hurt, you are weak; you are not weak when you do cry.

Yes, you read it right. Read it again. You may be wondering "Amir, how does that make sense?" Here is the reason: If you fail to cry even when you so deeply want to, it is then when you are considered weak because you are afraid to show your emotions; you are afraid of being judged by others; you are afraid to be yourself; you are afraid of being considered "weak" by people around you; you don't have enough self-esteem and self-confidence to show your real emotions. So what you do is you hide, you go away and cry on the inside, or you cry where there is no-one to see. You let all the emotions build up inside of you and it makes you a bitter person. Cry when you need to.

In the poem, I also briefly discuss the perception many people and society as a whole put on the level of honor a person deserves based on the type of work he/she does. Being a man/woman of integrity, values, and character is not determined in your career, but in how we carry ourselves in what we do, how we carry ourselves in life.

—⁓⌇⌇⌇⌇⌇⁓—

I wake up
Every single day
Blessed
With a prayer in my breath

Will this be the day?
That I finally glaze
The illusion society has made
Of the definition of strength

I was called weak
Said I'm not a man
Because I shed tears in a bleak
Bleak state of mind
Fighting for what was mine
My dreams
All I ever worked for
What I prayed for
Since I was a child

But in a matter of moments
Boom, it was gone

How could it be
That shedding tears for your love and idolatry
Is somehow considered as being weak
It's not like I've never been to war before
Not like I've never a held a gun before
Not like I've never shook the snobs before

Practicing law
I go to war every day
I show up
Put on my shackles
Like a predator
Looking for the prey

Gotta deal with the crooked cops
Filthy lawyers
And a bribed judge
But never have I shed a tear
Never will I budge
Call me weak again
Let's see what you got

I was called weak
Thought I was under his feet
Lord have mercy on their souls
For I can't call this a dream

Honor, isn't in what you do
It's how you apply yourself
The only thing, that dignifies the self!

"Letting go"

Topic: Letting someone go when necessary.

Sometimes, as hard as it is, we must simply let go. This concept applies to relationships, a job, a city we live in, or anything else in life we are holding on to and don't let go. I know I have preached about going with your instinct; and I am also a big believer of not giving up. But sometimes it is truly wasted energy. Now if your gut tells you that you should not let go of something, then refer to what I wrote in the paragraph discussing the poem "Different than the rest", and don't give up. But if your gut tells something is not right, as much of a dedicated and go-getter personality you may have, sometimes we must simply let go. Now I understand knowing whether we should let go of something or remain persistent can be hard, and sometimes we don't know what our gut or instinct is telling us, but when you do, then don't think twice. Prayer often helps tremendously when stuck in the confused state of not knowing whether to let go or remain persistent.

I have already written about a failed prior relationship which was a draining experience for me, and I kept trying to make it work. But had I let go much sooner than I did, things would have been a lot easier for me. I don't regret how I handled things, but I did learn from it.

Sometimes it is best to love from a distance. Love is not in being close physically, but it is about how close we are to that person in our hearts.

The frames on the wall clinging tightly
Pictures of love
Pictures of joy
Circling the fields of bluebonnets
Under the sunrays full of hope
Standing mightily!

We are wild, still wild
The distance is nugatory
Our hearts
Only a few second apart
Coming back together
Stronger, untouched
That type of love
Frames can't break apart

This is all obligatory
Rising with every beat
Every touch
Yet from afar
We see ourselves grow
Let our hearts shine

You may be lost
Seeking the arrays
But without a doubt
Only the hearts
Suffice!

Let the energy glow
Let it pick you up

Let it promise
The universe supports us
With every feeling
Recognized!

It's time to let go
Time to heal
Let our inner child
Forever take the wheel
To let you be
Let you see
That this love is real
Made of steel
To let you feel
Let me kneel
I'll by your side
In every moment you need

Moments of joy, stuck in a frame
Stuck only for a while
Moments of battles
Moments of war
Temporarily taking your soul
I'll be there to give you mine

Never doubt
Never forget
That letting go is hard
But what we need
To touch the sky

Remember always
I'm letting go
Only of your physical presence
Physical touch
But never letting go of love
That's in our hearts

Fly angel, fly
I'll by your side
For when you fall
Never will you fall
I've seen you ROAR
You've become so incredible
Time to get more

Letting go because I love God
I trust God
I love you
I love us
But clinging tightly will be the frames on the wall
That won't budge

Awaiting moments
Capturing new waves
Awaiting patiently
To dust the rust

"Hey you"

Topic: Love.

This is one of the earlier poems I wrote, and it is simply about adoring someone.

Hey you
Whose ideas I adore
I'm less hopeful without you
And when you're not around
I feel blue

Hey you
You always open the door
Sitting by the doorstep
Holding roses
Eshgh yani hamin[1]
Feeling really poor
It's you I adore

My tomorrow is unpredictable
But my today is fine
Mutual understanding

---

[1]   Farsi for "this is what love means".

Pure definition
Of a love divine.
Patiently waiting
For your hands in mine

Hey you
Stand up
And put your hands in mine.
Together we'll go far
Further than the sun
Eshgh yani hamin
Until the end of time
We will run
And always bond

"Crazy thoughts in my head"

Topic: Mental illness.

The extreme amount of attention by society on "physical health" and almost nonexistent lack of attention on "mental health" is alarming. Mental health leads to physical health significantly more than physical health leads to mental health. What do you hear everybody say when a person is going through a low point in life? Work out, go to gym, do something you like, hang out with family and friends, etc. Unfortunately, even most therapists or mental health professional also give the same meaningless advice on strategies to cope with mental health. We almost never hear anyone say, "practice co-dependency, practice different growth techniques, try somatic therapy, learn meditation, learn different breathing techniques." What do schools do for kids having difficulties learning worthless subjects like Algebra? They include P.E. to de-stress. There is no school curriculum to teach students mental health and self-improvement techniques; to teach students how to grow emotionally or mentally.

What happens when someone is mentally and emotionally happy? They are more likely to work out, enjoy life, etc. But what happens when someone has a mental disease and uses exercise to deal with it? It either gives a temporary minimal fix until the mental sickness takes over again, or the person simply cannot continue to exercise after a few sessions; the mental health issues and its roots never get addressed this way. Suicides have been on the rise in this country, including in children and young adolescents. The reasons are many, but in my opinion mainly because of lack of education on the subject, which is correlated to the lack of affordable access and government funding for mental health treatment.

While I was working for the Texas House of Representatives in Austin, I worked with a congressman who has always been a wonderful proponent in raising awareness in mental health issues; his name is Garnet Coleman (great man). I want to thank him for his services in this subject and hope we get more people in office like him.

These crazy thoughts
Won't leave me alone
Screaming!
What do they want?
It's late at night
And I can't sleep

Haven't had any alcohol in awhile
Months and years
But in my head
I'm drunk

Got so many blessings
I can't keep up
I can't count
Yet
My crazy mind tells me I'm cursed
My body
Not going along with the mind
Feeling fine
But the mind?
Terrified, anxious, chest tight!

Lord save me
From this internal fight
Tired of the voices in my head
Telling me about giving up
I tell them to "fuck off"
"What the fuck do you want?"

Can't they see that I'm fine?
I'm more than fine!
Tell them to go
And leave me behind
Tell them
I'm forever survived!

"Conspicuous thoughts of life"

Topic: Struggles of life and lack of compassion.

This is related to war, to broken hearts, to hopelessness, the increased lack of compassion in society, and so much more. It can be interpreted as you wish. For me, it's about taking a step back, smelling the roses, and appreciating all that we have been given. To have gratitude for every moment this precious life gives us. There are people who have it much worse.

———∿∽◦⌒◦⌒◦∽∿———

What do we do when we hurt?
Another glaze and march
What do we when we hurt?
Stories of love
Happiness, hope, broken

Another heartache in our lives
We have just been forsaken

We got it bad,
We got it bad cuz we see children bleeding,
Got it bad
Cuz there aint no air to be breathing,
Tired of trying, hoping, forgetting and forgiving,

When reality checks in
Love has been sleazing

No more sorrow
No more pain
Is what I wish for
when I see the rain, breezing
No more marching
It aint worth trying,

We are all sacrificing

Let the games begin
One by one
As we go down
One by one

Further than imagined
The story of love
In a room full of gowns
The gowns are there to be worn
So why don't we stop the bleeding
And let the champagne pour?

Maybe it's just how we are as humans,
Moving on
As we let love go
We might as well be ... nothing at all

"The broken lights"

Topic: Persistence.

I always pray for persistence. To me, persistence is an endangered human quality, nearing the level of going extinct. With the law rapidly evolving, and increased police power and government control, people are almost scared these days to be persistent. Although persistence can be applied in all aspects of life, I meet so many people in my office who have been charged with harassment charges for simply pursuing someone they like, or trying to keep a relationship together. While I don't agree with harassment and I am by no means advocating for harassment, I think we have become too sensitive. I am a young person, but even I have lived in a time when things were conducted "old fashioned." If you liked a girl, you would write letters, followed her without her noticing just to see her, left notes on her car door/window, stood somewhere she walked by just to get a glimpse of her, anonymously sent her flowers, etc. Now these behaviors are mostly considered "harassment." Most of the time a person doing these things would be considered "crazy." I believe a big part of the reason we now consider these behaviors as "harassment" is the improvement of technology. In an age where it is so easy to send text messages, voice messages, GIFs, memes, etc, in so many different platforms and apps, behaviors that should not be considered harassment have fallen victim to the increased awareness of harassment.

I remain a believer and activist of persistence. Do not let society and fear control who you are. Don't break the law and respect other people and their boundaries, but be persistent and try all that you can until there is nothing left, or you reach your goal.

The poem may not be directly viewed about the subject of persistence, but that is my view of it when I wrote it and the reader can have different meanings to it.

Walking through the streets
Bang, bang, goal!
Winning, hustling, running
With nothing else to do
I've been thinking, reminiscing
Should I break them?
No, not worth it

As a child, questioning sages
Do I know astuteness?
Or are they just oblivious?
Learning, living, hurting,
With broken lights in the streets
Still leering

Bang, bang, bang,
I heard them
Without appreciation
Doing what I do
And they seem so innocent
Stepping on the shattered glass

Inside homes
Through the doors
With their unruffled clothes
Getting out to join the boys

It's on again
Bang, bang, goal!
But this time
I hear shatters
Broken lights
All over the field
Damn!

Yet
We keep going
Not giving up
With our bloody feet
This is all we got

Broken lights won't stop me now
Darkness and pain
Try to keep me down
I take a deep breath
Envision, my thoughts
Darkness and pain
Are only in our minds

"Politics and gangs"

Topic: The significant power of money and the similar role it plays in politics and gangs.

Politics, gangs, I think they're both the same. Same agenda, same goals, just perceived differently.

Noises in the room
Loudly and clear
Tires screeching
Powder in the air

Shots fired
It's as foggy as it gets
Hiding as they shoot
But no-one can see them

Take the pain away
Only for a while
Blood and tears
Is only what they saw

Dripping and they fall
Rolling on the road
Another one goes down

Count it and blast
Count it to the game

Red over blue, blue over red
Cashing checks clear
Don't matter what they say
Money
Is what they chase

And red over blue, blue over red
With gunfights in the air
Crips take the gain
Bloods make them regret

Left wing and right wing
We call them parties
Protecting our rights
Empty handed they trail
Fuck it, let it rain

Crips and bloods apart
On the other side
Protecting our rights
Only in different ways
Fuck it, let it rain

Red over blue, blue over red
Significant signs
Of tears and despair
Call like it is
Call this shit insane
Suffer while they play

Across the view
Pointed on the wall
Sadness and sorrow
Push dreams afar

Take the pain away
Take it really far
Make them regret
What they know they've done
Make them wonder why

Rain can wash the scene
Rain can wash the pain
But only with money
Can this be a breeze

Dig deep and focus
Money's what they want
Punches in the air
Money all they want
Money all they got

Unity and collaboration
Doesn't cost a dime
Make them pay for it
Only with a smile

"Taxi driver"

Topic: The purpose of everyone we meet in life, however temporary.

I once met a man in my home country of Iran, the city of Tehran. I randomly met him as he was my taxi driver while I was out at night. I will call him X because of privacy reasons. I got a little bit sick when I was out trying to watch a show at the theatre. I was late to the show and I was not allowed to get in. Since I was sick, I decided to not wait for my uncle who was at the show to get out and meet his wife for the first time, I had to take a quick ride back home and meet his wife later. I even lost the money my uncle and his wife spent on the tickets. We were going to Uber but I told my cousin I needed to get home ASAP and couldn't wait for Uber since I was sick. After X picked me up, he said his direction was opposite of my home and had to drop me off to find a new taxi. I offered a certain amount of money if he took me anyways. He accepted with so much happiness. I could have easily found another taxi, but something told me to stay in that taxi, that all the events prior to that all were lined up for me to be with X.

On the 40-minute ride home, he told me a lot about his life. I noticed a broken hand. He told me he broke it a few months back and it costs too much money for surgery, and that he's also afraid of surgery. So, the doctors just wrapped it up hoping it heals. X did cabinet installation work and now he couldn't. Since the time it broke, his hand has been dislocated 3 times and he had popped it back in himself all 3 times. His car was old and ready to die. He was 33 but there was so much more in his face. We talked more and he told me about how at 11 years old, he had to leave home to work, as his family was struggling. He had lived alone since he was 11. A few years prior to meeting him, X used all his life savings of 20 years to complete this building project that took 2 years to complete, only to not get paid a dime at the end, since he didn't have a signed contract with the project manager. Since all his money was gone, the only love of his life, his love of 7 years, left him upon her dad's demand. X went into deep depression and for 6-7 months he only stayed home. When I met X, he was slowly getting back on his feet, working with the hope of something good in the future to happen. At the end of the ride, I gave him 4 times the amount I originally told him I would pay, which he was already extremely happy and grateful for. The look on his face looked like the world had changed and finally someone did him good. His happiness was priceless. I almost cried.

I decided to write a poem about X. We kept in touch after meeting him. But the morale of the story is everyone we meet in life, we meet for a purpose. Even if it is for a brief time, even if it is simply a smile as we pass by, or a simple hello. All events in life happen for a reason. Never get disappointed if you didn't make your show in time. Never be angry if you lose money on something you paid for and couldn't get a refund. This doesn't mean that you don't try to get your money back, but don't let anger take over, money always comes and goes. And don't be sad when you are sick.

I learned that soon after I met X, only a couple of days later, he went to go and see his family, his mom, after a very long time. I can say that losing a little bit of money, not being able to watch the show, getting sick for a couple of hours, and not being able to meet my uncle's wife for the first time (no offense to my uncle's lovely wife), were all worth it for me to be able to change someone's life. For a mom to finally see his son after a long time. For someone out there to have hope. And none of the events that were meant to happen but didn't for me to meet X, would have made for such a beautiful story as meeting X, which I will always carry with me for the rest of my life.

Get to know everyone you meet, help in any way you can, and always be thankful for everything that happened and didn't happen. We are one world, give love. Lastly, I am not surprised the sickness I had that night, even though it was severe, was the shortest lasting sickness I had ever experienced in my life. I was completely fine when I got home.

I once met a man
On a crowded and starry night
A man with a million unspoken words
Pushed behind the walls
Crucifying and unforgiving walls
That society had built up

No-one would entertain
In their busy and selfish lives
The secrets of a thousand miles
Countless, restless nights
With mistreatments and scars
Traveled by this lonely
Hopeless man afar

The dirty walls were unseen
To simple eyes
Or ordinary looks

You see,

To see what was behind
One must dig deep and be
Judgment free
Let's rewind

On this starry night
Were so many stories
So many lifestyles
From poor to rich
Lonely to bright
Happy and entertained
To depressed in fright
Soldier to knight
On every street corner stood
Someone selling a good
Just to make a buck

I was feeling a little down
Noises in my stomach
Body temperature rising
In the crowded town
Borderline complete collapse
I stood
Waiting for a cab

The taxi driver, this man
Was destined to be on my path
Without a doubt or lapse

I thought I had seen it all
The skinny child settling for a dime
The single mother carrying the load
So, her children can take a better road

Or the table with barely any food
Surrounded by conversations
No-one misunderstood

Yet the story of this lonely man
The almost hopeless man
Had me feeling shook
Feeling as if
I lacked gratitude
For this man, I became a fan

You see, this man had been through hell
Since 11 years old
He was destined to spend
His time, sweat
Scars and pain
So all of us can learn
We must bend but not break
We must appreciate

Leaving his family behind
At 11 years old
To be on his own
And go through it alone
So he can live and tell
The story for ages
A story to change the tale

For a decade he worked
His blood and sweat, he poured
For a life without worry, he explored

But the thieves and wolves, were bored
For their next victim, they torched

This man's hard work for years
He earned while dropping tears
The thieves and wolves mercilessly burned
Every last penny he zealously earned

Now with nothing left in his name
His love of 7 years

The only hope he had left
Had to leave him in tears

Because according to her dad
A man without a plan
A man with no money in the bank
Is not a man to keep around

As I looked at the sky
With tears in my eyes
I asked the one above
The only One who could shine
His blessings and divine
Wonders on anyone
To bless this man's soul
To bless his life

I also asked for:

Forgiveness and mercy
For everyone, mercilessly thirsty
Ruining other lives
So they can live in safety
I prayed for some compassion
And everyone to give graciously
Or at least to live courteously

As I left my ride
With the few dollars inside
I gave this man a smile
So big he couldn't hide

"Too fast"

Topic: Moving too fast in a relationship.

It's not always a bad thing.

For over thirty years
I prayed every day
I prayed to find
A reason to celebrate
This life I've been given
Let me illustrate:

While family and friends think
That I've gained it all, everything I ever I want
A job which provides
A chance to help someone survive
And to fight for justice, nonstop
Using the passion in my blood

———

And at the same time be
Financially stable and satisfied

First class trips, I can take
To any place in the world, in a sec
Friends in every industry I see

I can count on, for anything I need
I'm blessed, let it sink

A beautiful home, I got
A fancy car, I drive
Money for rainy days, not a problem
Luxury lifestyle, I can't hide them
With my office everyone impressed
Sunlight and blessings, got me possessed

And so much more I've been given
In all these years, I've been winning
Achieving success, in all things I've been doing
Trying to find happiness, pursuing

But the more I gained
The less happy I became
Realizing
It's you that I've missed

So when you tell me:
"I think you're moving too fast"
Please understand
That in your eyes, in most people's eyes
100% accurate you are
But in my eyes:

I'm moving too slow
In my eyes
It's been over thirty years
And another day to wait
Is like waiting a thousand years

You see, before I found you
At least I didn't know
That someone like you exists
Ignorant, I had nothing to miss

But after I was lucky enough
The answer to my prayers
Finally came up
Your presence
Had me in awe

So excuse me for the misunderstanding
That when it was time to go
And the only thing on my mind
Was an innocent kiss

With patience, perseverance, not giving up
It was you, I knew, since the first day we talked
So don't let another day go by
Without taking advantage
I might die

And if for a split second you think
After all these years of seeking
To find you and now I've almost reached it
That I'll just give up or leave that easily
You better think again, you're mistaken

And while, you may think we're moving too fast
Remember the words I said in the past
I've waited for thirty years
To reach this moment at last

So another day you wait
Another decision for you to make
Pondering the level trust I should get
For God's sake
Is another day gone to waste

Don't get me wrong you see
Even though it may seem
That I'm now asking for an increase in pace, or speed

Inaccurate perception that would be
As I wrote in the poem called "space", please read

I respect your timing to say
When the time is right, whether I can stay

"Sociopath"

Topic: Sociopaths and being "victimized" or a "survivor" of their cruelty.

Have you ever met a sociopath? Until recently, I considered the term very loosely. I did not believe that there were such crazy people in the world who would prey upon the kindhearted to get a sense of power, to reach their own ugly agenda. I now know I was mistaken. I have personally been victimized by a sociopath. I say "victimized" because that is the term society uses for those who have been targeted by sociopaths. However, I don't consider it that. And I think it's important that if you have ever been a target of a sociopath, to not consider yourself a victim. This is exactly what the sociopath seeks to achieve: to make you feel like you are the victim, thus they get a sense of power. I like to consider it being a "survivor." One of the definitions of "survivor" by Cambridge dictionary is "someone who is able to continue living their life successfully despite experiencing difficulties." That's all there is to it, you are a survivor, not a victim. Being a victim means you are hurt, being a survivor means you overcame the hurt someone or something tried to inflict upon you.

Every life experience is a lesson. Until recently, I did not believe in the existence of sociopaths as we define them. Now I am aware. I've learned not to easily give my trust to someone, no matter how good that person looks on the outside, no matter how amazing they may initially make you feel by their superb acting skills. The hard thing is usually a sociopath has all the apparent characteristics of an amazing person; thus, we fail to initially see them for who they are. Generally, they are good looking, talented, smart, charismatic, convincing, etc. But what is behind all that is a person with complete lack of empathy or compassion. Someone who is only concerned about themselves and their own agenda, even if it comes at the expense of playing with someone else's emotions. They take you to the peak of feeling truly amazing, and drop you in the shadow of darkness, without reason, without explanation, cold turkey. You may go from being extremely close to being completely ghosted by them in less than 24 hours, for no good reason, without a conversation. I am thankful for these people though. We should be thankful to them for not allowing us to spend more time feeling fake love. We should be thankful they did not allow us to be stuck with them on our journey of becoming the best, our journey of finding someone who we truly love and get reciprocity in return.

This one is for all the sociopaths out there and their survivors. Sociopaths, stop it, you are only hurting and disrespecting yourself. And survivors, remember to be thankful, remember you are a survivor not a victim.

You chase, making my heart race
Then you pull, break it apart like a toy
You run, without even saying goodbye
Return, temporarily to play some more
Then boom, you disappear on a broom
A witch, hidden behind your face, ugly soul
A game, you play to sense power within
Ashamed, You're a fool, surreal

I search, for what the heck happened and why
A torch, ignites my brain and I cry
Anger, dripping down my neck into the spine
And tense, sensations fill my every bone
Blown, to know a psychopath I chose
Intense, feelings all over my joints

Needing just a bit sense of power
They look for their next target to taunt
Make 'em scream louder, forever haunt
Victims with nightmares, while leaving their sight
They feel they can't do wrong
They're always mistakenly right

Be careful of these people I speak
Sociopaths, narcissists, or any terms we teach
Of these heartless men and women
They target the weak
For they know the vulnerability of the kindhearted, they can reach
They attack, hungry for power they proceed
Get your hopes up, then get you on your knees
Amazing on the outside but inside they reek!

—wwooeroorooww—

"Appreciate life"

Topic: Gratitude for everything we've been given.

When you need to be thankful, just look at the sky, clouds, trees, and see all the miracles given to us daily that we take for granted.

This life,
Full of blessings, it provides
Sunshine and majestic skies
Sometimes baby blue, orange, purple, and dark
Elegantly filled with bright stars
Blinking at us every night
Quietly saying everything is alright
Life goes on, no matter what's is our hearts
Or filled our minds with conflicting thoughts

Figuratively speaking, I say
Pretty birds in the dawn
They never miss the time
To awaken us, like alarms
—

As the king of the night
The full moon humbly steps aside
To let the red giant, the sun
Appear generously to let us shine

Appreciation for every moment we get
On this amazing planet, we call earth
Gratitude for everything we taste
Even in hard times we must give praise
Because there's no shame
To be in darkness or pain
Only through struggle, we find rest

So, stop and take a few steps
Back, relax, and demonstrate
Inner happiness, without hate
For the life we have, could end
In any moment, any place

"Fear"

Topic: Not allowing fear to overcome us.

Sometimes we get an opportunity so wonderful that we can't believe it is real. So, we allow fear and doubt start to cross our body and minds. Next thing we know fear has taken over and destroyed something amazing. Remember to always expect something amazing. If we live life expecting nothing amazing will happen to us, when it does, we will not be ready for it, we will think that it's not real, and allow fear and overprotection take over as opportunity passes right before our own eyes.

Fear fills your mind
Like a scattered child
Pertaining to lack emotions at all
Better retry

I got more wisdom than you give me credit
So, participate and anticipate
A break-though
A new hit

Inability to open up
You turn into a rock
Deep inside, you're still a rose
Inside that speechless and still stone

A pearl back into its shell
Like the turtle stuck on the road
Left broken and torn
Back into defense mode

All I ask, give me a chance
Don't let this opportunity pass
For this can forever last
It's all fears of the unknown,
Fears of the past

There's only so much stance
Left in my plans
To show you the amazing life we can have
And if you see I was wrong, at last
I'll happily walk away and bounce
And give someone else the last dance!

"Ghosted"

Topic: Ghosting someone, or in other terms, stonewalling.

We are all entitled to communication. If someone upsets you, tell them. If you don't want to be with someone, tell them. Don't take the easy way out to avoid the confrontation or conversation simply because you don't want to deal with the feelings associated with it. Ghosting them is much worse. Not only by ghosting you are showing your own weakness, you are also hurting someone else and basically telling them they don't even deserve a conversation. Obviously, the person you are ghosting had some significance in your life at some point, otherwise you would not be ghosting them.

Unfortunately, in today's world ghosting has become much easier because people can just hide behind their phones. It is not acceptable behavior.

No more waiting
No more pain
The confusion kills me
Let me explain:

You see, every moment I wait
Just to get a glimpse of your name
Awaken my phone
Is another year, flushed, torn
Every moment I wait
Another year goes by, another hair turns gray

And I would have been fine
Going a lifetime, to see you call
But all I wanna know
Is will it finally come?
The answer to which you fail to provide
You fail to give the reasons why
You're the only one now who can try
To clarify, what we got, change the outcome

I tried every road I could
Knocked on every door I could
Worn myself out, for you I should
It's how I'm built
But regrets in pouring my heart out
Fail to exist

Now it's your turn to stop the bleeding
Make a move and let's stop this nonsense
It's torturing me, and you know it
Neither of us deserves this

But I should take my own advice
As I mentioned before
"If someone is confused
And won't discuss or refuse
Ignores as if repeatedly hitting snooze
Let them be and remain confused"

It breaks my heart
Truth is I miss you so much
Wanna give up

But these feelings won't budge
Make it stop
My thoughts are going wild
Ok, goodbye

"Where Did You Go"

Topic: Same as previous poem, ghosting someone, or in other terms, stonewalling.

Just don't do it.

Fireworks in the air
Body filled with emotion
Telling me to wait
Before again you leave it broken

This is extremely unfair
Likely beyond repair
But my love won't go away
It's time to end this game
So call a timeout
And stop the play

So many messages I sent
So many calls I made
Please tell me how you feel
And if you're okay
Or just say it's over

Tired of wondering if you're okay
Tired of thinking when will be the next

Time, to call, to hear you say hello dear
Stop, rewind
Let's get to the end of the show, for real

Tired of hearing people telling me "it's okay"
Telling me to let it go, "aren't you ashamed?"
Ashamed I am, but I'm just a man
I care about, my life and plans

And currently, you got it all on hold
With nowhere to go
I can only be bold
But too much boldness
Can be mischievous
It can be evil
Destructive patterns
Can be heinous
Can turn legal

Telling me to trust you
It's all but faded
Give you some time to reflect
But not a word has been stated
To all the messages I sent
The flowers I sent

My heart, I must protect
I know it's hurting you too
Stop trying to play it cool
Stop pretending
As if it doesn't bother you a bit

For God's sake, just say it's over
Before I end my time of being sober
My mind is going wild, this is torture
I'm not one to give up, without closure
Not one to leave, without proper notice

The universe works in mysterious ways
What you're doing to me
Can teach you humbling lessons
God forbid, give you grueling fears
Or sadness filled with tears

Nightmares, in unlimited means
Humbling experience, just attack the scene
Tell me how you feel, let's be real
It ain't that hard, either speak or forever leave

When it's you who must face
The same confusion, and goes crazy next
You will remember the words I said
Seek forgiveness through prayer
Wishing the situation, you handled
With so much more care

"Worth the wait"

Topic: Waiting for a special someone, for true love.

Sometimes it's worth waiting for someone; no matter what each article online tells you. The typical "if they are not loving you back, never look back", cannot be applied to every situation. It's okay to wait sometimes.

Still thinking of you
Wanting to hold your hands
Tell you it's gonna be okay
Tell you, together we will never be gazed

Yeah, it's me again
Still thinking of you nonstop
Looking for your footprints to find
Your path, your destiny
Carry you when you're blind
Carry you when you're down

But still, your photos, all I have
As I take another glance
Every time I have the chance
To be reminded of your beauty, your class

Everywhere I look, I see memories of you
Your beautiful hair
The memories that won't die
Memories that won't go away

And never have I loved
So deep, so unconditional
Without a word or action by you, in response
Going wild, yet staying claim

I know eventually, you will come back
I know this isn't the end
Even if it's to say goodbye
Or to say "baby, I'm forever back", let's re-try
Hoping for the latter
I'll take my chances and wait
Because a person like you
Comes once in a million years
It's worth the grueling wait

To others, it may sound crazy and insane
But to me
To have the possibility to have you again
And forever remain
And not give it a try or wait
Is crazy and insane

You're worth the wait
No questions raised
Even if it includes pain
Or leaves me forever slain

———ᴍᴏᴀᴇᴛᴏᴏᴛᴇᴏᴏᴍ———

"Self-growth"

Topic: Happiness through self-improvement and growth, versus through material success.

We live in a world that material success is what defines success. However, what I've learned personally during the thirty plus years I have lived on this earth is that material success does not give happiness. I am thankful that God has blessed me with almost everything I have ever wanted, but happiness, true happiness comes in two forms only: 1) Serving others, and 2) Consistent self-improvement. If you think material success will give you happiness, you will never be happy.

Continuously seeking better ways
In improvements, we seek brighter days
Restless and overwhelmed
In Case
Opportunity comes, and we move to the next stage

Like shadows in daylight, out we phase
Losing ourselves in the chase
Seeking happiness in allusive ways
Material things and pointy tails
At night, we seek rest to replace
The energy used chasing, in the race

Seeking pleasure in all the wrong places
Chasing our own tails
With nonsense temptations
For things we assume give intense
Sensations of success, hallucinating pleasure and tears

Time, we don't get in unlimited doses
Guaranteed to run out at some point
Let's turn our focus
Seeking material success
From feverish sources
Will leave you lacking and gagging
For answers and solutions

Legacy, what I pray to reach
Lessons in life, advice, I tend to seek
Things I'm aiming to achieve
Self-love, emotional control, what we must teach
Without those, a pointless life, we live and preach

This life, and all the things we add up
We don't take to grave; we can't pack them up
So throw a smile next time you're down and out
You never know when you can once again, hash it out

"If today was your last"

Topic: Taking everything in perspective.

Life is extremely short. Take things in perspective. Are you doing things that you want to do? Do you know what is important in your life?

If today was your last
Would you finally stand
Tell your loves ones how much they mean to you
And forget the past?

If today was your last
Would you have the courage
To say what's on your mind
To fight for what's right
Or would you once again just casually pass?

If today was your last
Would you help the poor with your helping hands
Make a meaningful contribution to the world
And at the end of the road
Seize your last chance?

If today was your last
Would you spend time with your mate

Forget everything you hate
And be thankful for all that you have?

If today was your last
Would you travel the world
Would you book a last minute event
Attend your favorite show
Or would you lie down in your bed and remain sad?

If today was the end
Would you die as a kind soulmate
Or the one who broke hearts
Didn't understand a thing, lacking compassion
Would you visit grandma and grandpa
To give them a kiss goodbye
Or give your cash
To the lonely homeless men and women
Or would you keep them in your pants?

Would you got to work with a smile
Or would it be another Monday you can't stand
Would it be around people you love
Or co-workers you don't even know names by heart
But as another face in the crowd?

If today was your last
Would you make it count
Would the music of life be on blast
Would it be in happiness or frowns
Would it be the day people will remember you by
Or one in which no-one got to see a glace?

Would you be playing games
Thinking there will be another chance
Or would you seize the opportunity given
End it in a soft prayer
Speak what's on your brain, or your heart
Share your emotions, without care?

The answers to these questions
I won't share
But what guarantees
That today
Won't be your last?

Quotes

by me

"Dear Lord, forgive me for every night I went to sleep without gratitude, and every morning I woke up without saying hello to You!"

"Heartbreak is nothing but inspiration and passion to produce art."

"Be careful, there are many sociopaths out there who look great on the outside and are really good at acting. They often find victims to try to destroy so they can get a sense of power; they're dangerous."

"All our choices come down to two options: love and fear! Choose wisely; I'm guilty myself!"

"I'm so confident that the road I'm taking will eventually lead me to you, that I'm disregarding all the road signs saying I'm going the wrong way. You may call it insanity, I call it faith!"

"If I can't handle you at your worst, I don't deserve you at your best. Bet you've never seen it written that way before."

"Being a person of integrity, values, and character isn't determined in one's career, but in how one carries him/herself"

"It never works when you idealize or worship someone; that place is only reserved for God!"

"Trust that everything is working out exactly as it should be!"

"Instinct, a forgotten yet incredible human power."

"Fall in love with someone's ideology, beliefs, and character; not for their behavior. People's behavior can sometimes fluctuate depending on their mood. We all have moments or times of being in a bad mood."

"Don't wait for the perfect person; wait for someone who has "excitement in her eyes when she talks about her goals. Someone who sings with her soul, plays music in a different world, and talks as if reciting poems. Someone who has been through hell lately but somehow still smiles, with so much strength continues to walk. Someone who makes dumb decisions sometimes because she just wants to make the world a better place. Who believes in herself to a level that amazes you and also knows how much you believe in her. Someone who knows her worth but knows that she has a long way to go. Someone with a story you desperately want to read and explore. Someone who knows she is a star and hasn't settled because she knows it would be a mistake; for she knows she deserves the best. She deserves someone who will be there for her when she needs it, but also gives her space when she wants to be left alone. Wait for someone who won't compromise her independence but will love you with all her heart and soul, when you gain her trust. Someone with kindness, boldness, and confidence in every inch of her heart."

"Not everything goes as we plan, learn to enjoy the unexpected!"

"If someone is confused about you, and won't communicate with you, let them be and remain confused. Find someone who is sure instead!"

"I write, when I'm dealing with something I write."

"It's a sin, letting someone take your joy. So pick up your chin. You deserve better, seek happiness from within. I see the world sometimes crumble. We go through it all. We all struggle. Yet, with all the bull shit I still smile. I laugh at it like a joke. And give a big nice "fuck you" when Satan tries to break me apart."

"I don't really care about disappointing anyone. If I have to worry about disappointing someone, they aren't important enough to begin with."

"Sometimes people are upset with you because you were a part of the reason they are upset with themselves, not because they are upset with you."

"We all just need to have more compassion for each other and understand."

"Everything, even things we may feel at the time are terrible beyond imagination, happen for a reason, for a much better reason!"

"You are not weak when you cry, you are weak when you want to cry but don't, to prevent from being judged by others."

"When you need to be thankful, just look at the sky, the clouds, trees, and all the miracles given to us daily that we take for granted."

"When someone apologizes, be human and brave enough to accept it. It doesn't mean you give them the same trust again. You accept the apology not only for that person, but also for yourself."

"Don't force love, accept heartache, and seek happiness
from within rather than other people or things."

"Struggle causes one of two things: depression or growth.
Choose growth! Choose to be a victor not a victim!"

"Behind the smile there are a thousand stories of struggles I've
overcome and still overcoming that most people have no idea about."

"A life fighting for justice and never reaching your goal is worth
way more than a life living in comfort accepting evil."

"No one wants to know about stories of people that were
given everything, they want to know about people who
endured pain, and turned it into something, something
BIG! Become a part of history, not live in misery!"

"Life can change in a matter of hours! Cherish it."

"Whatever worry we have, whatever stress we have, it's all
because of how amazing we are and how we want everything
to be so perfect. We are stronger than we think, we are more
capable than we think. So, relax, take things into perspective,
and enjoy life. We have everything under control."

"Think about the underlying potential possibilities
before your freak out about something, really think and
analyze; it automatically makes you less freaked out."

CPSIA information can be obtained
at www.ICGtesting.com
Printed in the USA
BVHW031035191219
567197BV00004B/23/P

9 781796 076363